IMAGES OF WAR

SS FOREIGN DIVISIONS AND VOLUNTEERS OF LITHUANIA, LATVIA AND ESTONIA 1941–45

RARE PHOTOGRAPHS FROM WARTIME ARCHIVES

Ian Baxter

Pen & Sword
MILITARY

First published in Great Britain in 2021 by
PEN & SWORD MILITARY
an imprint of
Pen & Sword Books Ltd
47 Church Street
Barnsley
South Yorkshire
S70 2AS

ISBN 978-1-39901-298-0

A CIP catalogue record for this book is available from the British Library.

Typeset by Concept, Huddersfield, West Yorkshire HD4 5JL
Printed and bound in England by CPI Group (UK) Ltd, Croydon CR0 4YY

FSC www.fsc.org MIX Paper from responsible sources FSC® C013604

Pen & Sword Books Limited incorporates the imprints of Atlas, Archaeology, Aviation, Discovery, Family History, Fiction, History, Maritime, Military, Military Classics, Politics, Select, Transport, True Crime, Air World, Frontline Publishing, Leo Cooper, Remember When, Seaforth Publishing, The Praetorian Press, Wharncliffe Local History, Wharncliffe Transport, Wharncliffe True Crime and White Owl.

For a complete list of Pen & Sword titles please contact
PEN & SWORD BOOKS LIMITED
47 Church Street, Barnsley, South Yorkshire S70 2AS, England
E-mail: enquiries@pen-and-sword.co.uk
Website: www.pen-and-sword.co.uk

Contents

About the Author

Ian Baxter is a military historian who specialises in German twentieth-century military history. He has written more than fifty books including *Poland – The Eighteen Day Victory March, Panzers In North Africa, The Ardennes Offensive, The Western Campaign, The 12th SS Panzer-Division Hitlerjugend, The Waffen-SS on the Western Front, The Waffen-SS on the Eastern Front, The Red Army at Stalingrad, Elite German Forces of World War II, Armoured Warfare, German Tanks of War, Blitzkrieg, Panzer-Divisions at War, Hitler's Panzers, German Armoured Vehicles of World War Two, Last Two Years of the Waffen-SS at War, German Soldier Uniforms and Insignia, German Guns of the Third Reich, Defeat to Retreat: The Last Years of the German Army At War 1943–45, Operation Bagration – the Destruction of Army Group Centre, German Guns of the Third Reich, Rommel and the Afrika Korps, U-Boat War,* and most recently *The Sixth Army and the Road to Stalingrad.* He has written over a hundred articles including 'Last days of Hitler', 'Wolf's Lair', 'The Story of the V1 and V2 Rocket Programme', 'Secret Aircraft of World War Two', 'Rommel at Tobruk', 'Hitler's War With his Generals', 'Secret British Plans to Assassinate Hitler', 'The SS at Arnhem', 'Hitlerjugend', 'Battle of Caen 1944', 'Gebirgsjäger at War', 'Panzer Crews', 'Hitlerjugend Guerrillas', 'Last Battles in the East', 'The Battle of Berlin', and many more. He has also reviewed numerous military studies for publication, supplied thousands of photographs and important documents to various publishers and film production companies worldwide, and lectures to various schools, colleges and universities throughout the United Kingdom and the Republic of Ireland.

Introduction

Drawing on a collection of rare and unpublished photographs, *SS Foreign Divisions and Volunteers of Lithuania, Latvia and Estonia 1942–45* tells how the Germans recruited conscripts into the Waffen-SS from those countries. It describes how Lithuania, unlike her Latvian neighbour, had no plans to provide Germany with a 'national legion of volunteers'. Although many volunteers came forward, most were absorbed into German-sponsored units. As for Latvia and Estonia, thousands were recruited into their own foreign legion – Waffen grenadier SS divisions – where they saw action around Leningrad, in the Ukraine, and in defensive operations in the Baltic States as the Red Army smashed its way through them in 1944.

Chapter One

Invasion and Occupation 1941–42

At dawn on 22 June 1941 approximately 3 million German soldiers on the frontier of the Soviet Union embarked on one of the most brutal conflicts of the twentieth century: Operation BARBAROSSA. Directing this invasion of Russia were Field Marshal Ritter von Leeb, commander of Army Group North, Field Marshal Fedor von Bock in the centre, and Field Marshal Gerd von Rundstedt in the south.

Army Group North was tasked with destroying the Red Army in the Baltic region. Hitler stipulated on the eve of the invasion that the objective was to thrust across East Prussia, smashing Soviet positions along the Baltic, liquidating the bases of the Baltic Fleet, destroying what was left of Russian naval power and capturing Kronstadt and Leningrad. Once those cities had been razed to the ground, the German armies could sweep down from the north while the main force closed in from the west. With 500,000 men at Leeb's disposal comprising thirty divisions, six of them armoured and motorized, with 1,500 tanks and 12,000 heavy weapons, plus a fleet of 1,000 planes, he was determined to dispose of the Russian force quickly and efficiently.

Leeb's force, consisting of the 16th and 18th armies, smashed easily through the Soviet defences on the first day. Russian soldiers stood helpless in their path, too shocked to act. Over the following weeks, troops of *Heeresgruppe Nord* smashed through enemy positions in Lithuania, Latvia and Estonia, straight towards their objective: Leningrad. The earth was baked hard by the summer sun and Leeb's army was able to advance rapidly.

When German troops advanced through the Baltic States to achieve their first strategic successes, thousands of Lithuanians, Latvians and Estonians volunteered to assist them. Many saw the Nazi invasion as the beginning of the destruction of the Soviet Empire. Within days of the attack, towns and cities across Lithuania were abandoned by the Red Army as German armoured vehicles moved into suburbs and were welcomed as liberators. Similar scenes of liberation were apparent in Latvia. In Riga, the Latvian resistance began street battles against Red Army troops.

Although the Germans proclaimed that the people of the Baltic States wanted to serve Adolf Hitler, the inhabitants of the three states were actually hoping for the independence of their countries. However, the people would soon realize that the Nazis were just another occupying power, pillaging the country for their war effort. Another nasty surprise was 'the Holocaust', the murder of thousands of Jews, Gypsies, Russians and Soviet prisoners of war.

Yet in spite of this barbaric crusade by the Nazis, across Latvia there were thousands of people that decided to aid the German war machine by joining German organizations and military units, including the Luftwaffe. In late July 1941, just a month after the German invasion of Russia, the Germans began recruiting an auxiliary police force (*Ordnungs-Hilfspolizei*) of approximately 3,000 Latvian men comprising five companies. The number of police units grew over the next few months. Some fought alongside front-line German army units in Russia, others fought partisans or carried out guard or logistical duties and some rounded up and killed Jews. Latvian military leadership and Latvian civilians in the German-appointed government pushed to merge these widely-dispersed police units into a larger all-Latvian combat force.

Yet, unlike her Latvian neighbour, Lithuania had no plans to provide Germany with a National Legion of volunteers. Although within weeks of the German occupation of the country there was a large volume of volunteers that came forward, the majority of them, as many as 50,000, were slowly absorbed into German-sponsored units. In fact, many volunteers were initially deserters from the Soviet 29th Light Infantry Corps. As for the other volunteers and conscripts that came forward during the initial stage of German occupation, they comprised numerous ad hoc units formed as the Soviets were retreating. For the most part, as in the other Baltic nations, these Lithuanian ad hoc units were disbanded once the German occupation was complete. In some cases, select units provided the basis for new self-defence formations formed by the Germans for security operations.

In Estonia, when the Soviets had retreated and the country was under German administration, there was a large-scale volunteer programme recruiting Estonian men in the ranks of the Wehrmacht. Although the majority joined the German army voluntarily, often out of the desire to fight the Soviet Union, most of the newly-drafted Estonians served in the rear of the Army Group North security until the early winter of the following year.

The use of the Baltic nations as recruits in the fight against 'Bolshevism' was still severely restricted in 1941. However, as the war on the Eastern Front dragged on through a terrible winter, with the front stagnating and the Red Army beginning to fight back, new recruitment measures were imposed to create military formations from races that were unequivocally non-Aryan.

Six photographs depicting the German invasion of the Soviet Union in June 1941. These troops are advancing through the Baltics in Army Group North. For the invasion of Russia, code-named BARBAROSSA, the German army assembled some 3 million men divided into a total of 105 infantry divisions and 32 panzer divisions. There were 3,332 tanks, more than 7,000 artillery pieces, 60,000 motor vehicles and 625,000 horses. This massive force was distributed into three German army groups. Army Group North, commanded by General Wilhelm Ritter von Leeb, had assembled his forces in East Prussia on the Lithuanian frontier. His force provided the main spearhead for the advance on Leningrad. In Army Group North the German army wasted no time and soon sliced through the bewildered Russian forces on every front. The ferocity and effectiveness of both the infantry and panzer divisions were so great that some of the Red Army forces either withdrew in panic or were surrounded and systematically annihilated in a hurricane of fire. Leeb's Army Group North was given the task of destroying the Red Army fighting in the Baltic region. Hitler stipulated on the eve of the invasion that the German objective was to thrust across East Prussia, smashing Soviet positions along the Baltic, liquidating the bases of the Baltic Fleet, destroying what was left of Russian naval power and capturing Kronstadt and Leningrad.

A German motorcycle unit during the invasion of the Baltics in the summer of 1941.

Two photographs showing the devastation wrought by the Wehrmacht on the Red Army as it swept through the countries of Lithuania, Latvia and Estonia. Leeb's force comprised the 16th and 18th armies.

(**Opposite, above**) Wehrmacht soldiers round up a group of Latvian civilians. In order for the occupation to run smoothly the Germans were eager for the creation of collaborationist organizations and the recruitment of military volunteers.

(**Opposite, below**) A 15cm howitzer being pulled by animal draught during the Wehrmacht's march through Lithuania in June 1941.

(**Above**) A column of German vehicles has halted and Lithuanian women can be seen giving water to the soldiers. After the Soviet occupation, many Lithuanians looked at the German invasion of their country as liberation.

A German motorcycle combination unit advances through a Lithuanian town which appears to have seen some ground or aerial bombing.

A photo taken from a still propaganda film showing a smiling German soldier offering a Latvian civilian a cigarette.

Inside the city of Riga and the local population hail the Germans as liberators from Soviet suppression. Little did the people know what was in store as the Nazi government took control of their country.

A crowd of Latvian civilians have gathered around a German vehicle in Riga following the Wehrmacht's entry into the city. The German soldiers smile as they are given food from a welcoming group of people, happy that they are free from Soviet control and rule.

(**Above**) Wehrmacht soldiers being greeted by civilians in the Latvian city of Riga. The occupation of Latvia by Nazi Germany was completed on 10 July 1941. Latvia became a part of Nazi Germany's *Reichskommissariat Ostland*: the Province General of Latvia.

(**Opposite, above**) In Riga and a German soldier hands out what appears to be propaganda leaflets to a passing motorcyclist combination. Note the vehicle with speakers. This was used through the streets of Riga to spread various government instructions to the local populace and spread propaganda. German propaganda emphasized the prowess of German arms and the humanity German soldiers had shown to the peoples of the occupied territories of the Baltic States.

(**Opposite, below**) Estonian nationalists march through the streets of Tallinn, triumphantly rejoicing that the city has been freed from Soviet rule. During June and July 1941 as the Wehrmacht rolled across the Baltic States towards the Estonian capital, pro-independence 'Forest Brothers' captured South Estonia from the NKVD and the Russian 8th Army before the arrival of the German 18th Army.

WH

(**Above**) A newly-recruited Lithuanian policeman can be seen in a village after he has rounded up a group of Jewish people. Almost immediately following the occupation of the Baltic States the *Reichskommissariat Ostland* ordered that the Jewish and Romani people be rounded up and sent to newly-created ghettos. However, many of them were systematically murdered by the *Einsatzgruppen* murder squads. It is estimated that 80 per cent of the Lithuanian Jews were killed before 1942, many by or with the active participation of Lithuanians in units such as police battalions. The surviving 43,000 Jews were concentrated in the Kaunas, Vilnius, Švenčionys, Šiauliai and ghettos and forced to work as slave labour for the Reich.

(**Opposite, above**) An Estonian Legion recruiting-point in 1941. Initially Estonian volunteers were recruited into the Wehrmacht to fight against the Red Army. They were known as so-called *Sicherungsabteilunge*. These ethnic Estonians were conscripted into the 8th Estonian Rifle Corps and fought alongside German units. They were created in Estonia and incorporated former officials of the Republic of Estonia's army.

(**Opposite, below**) Troops during a training exercise in 1941. The soldier is armed with an StG 24 hand grenade.

Meldestelle
ür Freiwillige der Legion Estland
Eesti Leegioni
atahtlikkude registreerimise pu

Chapter Two

Foreign Recruitment

By the spring of 1942 the German war machine had recovered from the Russian winter. Hitler, who was now in full command of operations on the Eastern Front, was determined to smash the Red Army once and for all. In Army Group North, all operational objectives through the Baltics, despite stubborn Red Army resistance and several unsuccessful counter-attacks, had been victorious. The Wehrmacht were now operating along the eastern shore of Lake Ladoga and had already surrounded the city of Leningrad in an attempt to starve the city into submission.

Elsewhere on the Eastern Front German units began pushing forward. In the south an offensive was mobilized with an objective to seize the oil fields in the Caucasus. Before that objective could be attained, an all-out drive was ordered south to capture a city called Stalingrad. Strategically Stalingrad was no Moscow, but to the Germans success of the summer campaign could not be claimed without its capture. Victory meant that the city would be used as an anchor in which Hitler could send the mass of his panzer force south to occupy the Caucasus.

However, within months the German divisions, notably from the 6th Army, became embroiled in a protracted bloodthirsty urbanized battle, which saw much of the southern front stagnated and fighting for survival.

Elsewhere on the Eastern Front, the situation had not improved. In Army Group Centre the front was more or less paralyzed, with many of its important units drained off to support the drive in the south. In Army Group North, their position had not altered and the city of Leningrad still remained defiant.

Fighting on all fronts continued throughout 1942, but at a considerable cost to Germany's manpower and resources. In order to compensate for the losses it was agreed to recruit units of non-Germanic descent. This recruitment programme included expanding the Waffen-SS. On 1 September 1942, the Waffen-SS had a field strength of 141,975 men with an additional 45,663 in training and reserve. Exactly a year later that figure had almost doubled to 280,000 in the field units and 70,000 in training and reserve. During this period of expansion the Waffen-SS for the first time had to resort to the large-scale conscription of foreign recruits. Thousands of youths who met SS standards were drafted from the work camps of the Reich Labour

Service. Nordic volunteers and *Volksdeutsche* (people of Germanic descent from countries in Eastern Europe) helped dilute the so-called pure Nordic stock with foreign blood.

On 23 January 1943, SS *Reichsführer* Heinrich Himmler received Hitler's approval to form a Latvian SS Volunteer Legion, which would eventually be comprised of two Waffen-SS volunteer divisions. Already extremely anti-Bolshevik, the Latvians mutually shared the Nazi objective of defeating the Soviets. However, for them, their greatest appeal of being a legion was not being allied with the Germans but a basis for building a national army that could one day restore Latvian independence. While some legionnaires were fascists, the majority had no illusions about their predicament of joining arms with the Nazis. Many of the volunteers were former members of the Latvian army or former policemen. For them, the legion provided an opportunity for redemption and revenge as well as the possibility of future independence.

In response to the recruitment programme, two Latvian police battalions were pulled from the front and trained along with a third. This new unit established an all-volunteer Latvian Legion and was quickly sent to the front lines to participate in the siege of Leningrad. It only saw minor action before it was again pulled out of the line. Weeks later, in February 1943, in an effort to expand the legion, the Germans created the *Lettische SS-Freiwilligen-Division*, which later received the numerical designation 15. The legion was renamed the *Lettische SS-Freiwilligen-Brigade*, with the numerical designation added soon after. Later it was designated the *15. Waffen-Grenadier-Division der SS (Lettische Nr. 1)* or the 15th Waffen SS-Grenadier Division (1st Latvian). Recruitment for the division was compulsory, and all Latvian citizens born between 1919 and 1924 were required to go to the recruitment station in Riga with their papers. Training was basic and the new recruits were quickly transported to the Eastern Front where they fought around Leningrad against superior Russian units. As they fought, a second Latvian SS Volunteer Brigade was formed and 1,000 untrained volunteers were sent to the front in the Leningrad sector. The area in which they operated comprised a series of lakes, rivers and mosquito-infested swamps that soldiers called 'the end of the world'. In the damp, dark, boggy and forested area the legionnaires constructed log roads and above ground log cabins and log fortifications that often flooded. Their relationship with the German military was also fragile and disagreements frequently occurred over poor training, inadequate equipment and the Latvians' craving for their Latvian officers to command the legion.

During the ensuing months, despite being undertrained, lacking proper weaponry and equipment, the 15th Waffen-SS Grenadier Division (1st Latvian) saw action in the southern sector of Leningrad next to the 2nd Latvian SS Volunteer Brigade.

In Lithuania, involvement in the war effort against the Red Army was much less. The Lithuanians were for the most part formed into auxiliary support units for security operations. The first formal unit to be formed was known as the *Lituanische*

Hunterschaften, which was later formed into a number of self-defence units known as *Selbschutz-Bataillonen*. The *Selbschutz-Bataillonen* units were later brought under the control of the German organization of uniformed front-line police, the *Ordungs-Polizei*, and renamed as *Schutzmannschaft-Bataillonenor Schumas*. In May 1943, the *Schuma* units were renamed and re-formed into *Polizei-Bataillonen*. Virtually all the units were formed in battalion-sized forces consisting of between 500 and 600 men each, primarily assigned to rear-area security duties.

Apart from these battalion-sized security units, there were also five *Lituanische Bau Bataillonen* numbered I to V that were formed during 1943. All five units were attached to German Pioneer units under the control of Army Group North. All the commanding officers were Lithuanian and their men were tasked with road and railway construction and the building of defensive positions. Initially the units were not armed, but as partisan activity became more active in the region, they were given a variety of light weaponry to protect themselves. Although these construction units were under control of the Wehrmacht, many members eventually joined the Waffen-SS, but no Lithuanian national unit was ever formed under the Waffen-SS and all volunteers served on an individual basis. However, for many months in 1943, the Lithuanian menfolk had been pressured to raise a Lithuanian Legion for the Waffen-SS. Even the German military administration governing the country threatened to put all able-bodied Lithuanians into labour camps until a compromise was reached. Yet despite these threats, the Lithuanians argued for an independent formation led by Lithuanian officers and not under the control of the SS.

In Estonia the recruitment programme increased and volunteers were pressured to join the SS in their hundreds. In late 1942, volunteers signed up for the SS Legion and by May 1943, the Germans had expanded the SS Legion to a brigade size, known as the Estonian SS Volunteer Brigade or *Estnische SS-Freiwillige Brigade*. The 1st SS Volunteer Regiment became the 45th SS Volunteer Regiment, and the 53rd Artillery Battalion was formed to support the brigade. A couple of months later, the 657th Estonian Company and 660th Estonian Battalion were used to help form the 46th SS Volunteer Regiment as the second regiment of the brigade.

In October, the brigade was renamed the 3rd SS Volunteer Brigade. The majority of its commanders were Estonian, including the two regimental commanders. Within weeks of its establishment the brigade reached a strength of 5,099 men. From late 1943, the brigade was committed to fighting partisans at Nevel near Velikiye in Russia. It then joined the German 16th Army north of Staraya.

In Russia other SS legions were also operating, including 800 men of a Volunteer Battalion Narva known as *Freiwillige-Bataillon Narva*. The new battalion was hastily sent to the Eastern Front where it joined the Nordic-recruited 5th SS Panzer Division *Wiking*, replacing a Finnish SS battalion. Volunteer Battalion Narva distinguished itself fighting as part of the 5th SS Division in the Ukraine.

A Latvian Waffen-SS recruitment poster. In January 1943, the Latvian Legion initially comprising Latvian police battalions was created on the orders of SS *Reichsführer* Heinrich Himmler. A month later German occupation authorities in Latvia started conscripting men of military age. Draftees were given a choice between serving in the Waffen-SS legions or in Wehrmacht auxiliaries. Those that did not volunteer were threatened with being sent to a slave labour camp in Germany or a concentration camp. As a result, less than a quarter of the men serving in the legion were actual volunteers. Unlike in Lithuania, the government in Latvia did not ban potential legionary recruits. However, some Latvians did desert rather than serve for the German military war effort.

An Estonian Waffen-SS recruitment poster. A number of Estonian volunteers fought in the German army against the Red Army in Russia and in the Ukraine from September 1941. A year later, following a recruitment initiative by the German Latvian authorities, the formation of the voluntary Estonian Legion was proclaimed on 28 August 1942 and the 3rd Estonian SS Volunteer Brigade was established. Some 500 volunteers had appeared and signed up for the legion by 13 October 1942. In the spring of 1943, additional men were drafted from the police forces and men born between 1919 and 1924 were conscripted into the Estonian Legion and the number rose to 1,280. By the spring of 1943, some 5,300 men were conscripted into the Estonian Legion and 6,800 for the support service of the Wehrmacht. Out of the conscripts was formed the second Estonian Regiment and the Estonian SS Volunteer Brigade was established on 5 May 1943.

Newly-created soldiers of the 15th Waffen Grenadier Division during a parade in 1943. This Latvian division was formed in February 1943. Initially it was known as the *Lettische SS-Freiwilligen-Division* and later received the numerical designation 15. The legion was renamed the *Lettische SS-Freiwilligen-Brigade*, with the numerical designation added soon after. The formations with volunteers of Germanic background were officially named *Freiwilligen* (volunteer), including ethnic Germans born outside the Reich known as *Volksdeutsche*, and their members were from satellite countries. These were organized into independent legions and had the designation *Waffen* attached to their names for formal identification. *(NARA)*

Members of the newly-recruited Waffen-SS Latvian Legion can be seen marching next to the Dome Cathedral in the capital city of Riga on Latvian Independence Day in 1943. *(NARA)*

A commanding officer during an inspection of his Estonian troops. They all wear the summer SS camouflage smocks and are armed with the Karabiner 98K bolt-action rifle.

Marching through Riga in the summer of 1943 are soldiers of the Latvian 15th Waffen-Grenadier Division 3.

Latvian recruits comprising Wehrmacht, Waffen-SS and Luftwaffe auxiliaries are seen here queuing to collect their supplies in 1943. *(NARA)*

Soldiers of the Latvian 15th Waffen-Grenadier Division 1 marching through Riga. *(NARA)*

Estonian SS recruits known by the German authorities as Germanic-SS or *Germanische-SS*, which was the collective name given to SS groups that were formed in occupied Europe including the Baltic States. The Germanic-SS were not raised as military units like the Waffen-SS, although many Germanic-SS members did join the foreign combat divisions. *(NARA)*

A Latvian SS soldier tunes the radio during Christmas festivities in 1943. *(NARA)*

A Latvian soldier during training wearing the M35 steel helmet and displaying the SS decal observes positions through a pair of 6 × 30 Zeiss binoculars. In fact, many of the volunteers that reported for training were surprised at the rigid discipline, the lack of living conditions and hard training of the SS. *(NARA)*

Latvian troops are getting accustomed to the antiquated PaK35/36 anti-tank gun, which by 1943 was often relegated to training soldiers. Many of the weapons that the Baltic SS troops received were often second-rate. *(NARA)*

A young Latvian recruit during a training exercise in 1943. The formation of the Latvian division went slowly in the conscription of men and officers. When the division was finally assembled and ordered to depart for the front, most of the soldiers had limited training. *(NARA)*

Latvian 15th Waffen-Grenadier Division 10 PaK crew during a training exercise under the watchful eye of *SS Reichsführer* Heinrich Himmler and his commanding officers. (*NARA*)

Himmler with his commanding officers observes a Latvian Grenadier SS PaK crew training on the edge of a forest clearing in 1943. Those that trained the Latvian recruits had little sympathy regarding the rigorous training they put them through. Many were bullied and mentally abused by their NCOs. (*NARA*)

Another photograph taken in sequence showing a young Latvian PaK gunner during a training exercise, while Himmler and his commanding officers observe. *(NARA)*

Latvian soldiers during a passing-out parade ceremony in 1943. Little did these soldiers know what was in store for them on the Eastern Front. Within a year these troops would be defending their homeland against a powerful and vengeful Red Army. *(NARA)*

A Latvian PaK crew during a training exercise. (*NARA*)

During training and men of the Latvian *Hundesstaffel* 61, or dog unit, can be seen during meal-time next to a small HF12 field kitchen wagon (*Feldküchenwagen*). These field kitchens provided the troops with soups, stews and coffee. The limber carried cooking utensils and equipment. (*NARA*)

At a forward observation post, troops can be seen trying to identify the enemy through their 6 × 3 Zeiss binoculars.

Six photographs showing a Latvian *SS-Infanterie* Brigade PaK crew during a training exercise. Their training is being observed by their NCO, which was often strict and gruelling. By the mid-war, with the growing might of Russian armour, many PaK guns were built for the front lines and utilized for both offensive and defensive operations. These trained PaK gunners would soon be used to defend their own country using these weapons. *(NARA)*

Latvian *SS-Infanterie* Brigade 1 during a training exercise in 1943. Their trainer can be seen holding a part of the Karabiner 98K rifle, which was often universally used by both German and non-German forces. *(NARA)*

An Estonian soldier clad in his winter whites during a reconnaissance mission in the late winter of 1943.

Soldiers belonging to the Latvian *Hundesstaffel* boarding a vehicle, probably to the front. Due to the lack of transport many commercial vehicles were handed over to the German authorities in Latvia and utilized for military purposes. (*NARA*)

Latvian soldiers have utilized their waterproof camouflage Wehrmacht-issue Zeltbahn capes to form protective covering between two stationary panzers. *(NARA)*

Latvian troops repairing their boots out in the field. Note the Zeltbahn waterproof cape has been erected as a tent in order to give some shelter to the soldiers from the sun. *(NARA)*

A column of Estonian grenadiers belonging to the 20th Waffen Grenadier Division of the SS (1st Estonian) hitching a lift on board vehicles. The division was officially activated on 24 January 1944, and many of its soldiers had been members of the Estonian Legion and the 3rd Estonian SS Volunteer Brigade, which had been fighting as part of German forces since August 1942 and October 1943. Both these formations drew their personnel from Estonia with widespread conscription announced by the German occupying authorities. The division was formed in Estonia around a cadre comprising the 3rd Estonian SS Volunteer Brigade and was initially known as the 20th Estonian SS Volunteer Division.

Troops being transported to the forward edge of the battlefield during operations in the summer of 1944.

Two photographs showing Latvian soldiers from the 15th Waffen Grenadier Division during a training exercise. Many of the foreign volunteer units of the Waffen-SS only reached regimental strength, despite being designated a legion or division, and also lacked the full support elements such as weapons, armour and other combat components that were usually associated with a premier SS division. The 15th Division order of battle comprised three infantry regiments, each with two battalions, an infantry howitzer company, an anti-tank company, an artillery regiment with four battalions, a reconnaissance battalion, an engineer battalion and respective supply units. *(NARA)*

Two photographs taken in sequence showing soldiers of the 15th Waffen-Grenadier Division pushing a field ambulance through a forest location in the Novosokolniki area in Russia. In November 1943, the Latvian volunteers saw action in this area, fighting hard against the Soviet winter offensive. However, most of the soldiers had on average only forty to sixty days of training, which is why there was a high casualty rate within their units. *(NARA)*

In a forest during operations in Russia and Latvian signalmen can be seen with cable reels obviously locating a good forward position. The signals soldier was nicknamed the 'line puller' or *Strippenzieher*.

From a position the relay post could talk to its platoons and the battalion headquarters by way of field telephones, as depicted in this photograph. Here they relayed messages from adjacent companies.

During the winter of 1943, and this Latvian soldier appears to be cutting frozen meat. The Latvian volunteers adapted well to their surroundings, especially in the harsh Russian winters.

A supply vehicle has slid off an icy track during operations in the Novosokolniki area. In November and December 1943 the Latvians' plan was to deploy all the divisional units to the immediate rear of the front in the Novosokolniki region, where they would gain experience in active combat under the command of the German 205th and 83rd Infantry divisions. *(NARA)*

Soldiers donned in their winter reversibles during operations in Army Group North in 1944. By this period of the war the stagnated front in the north was now under serious threat of being overrun by the Red Army as it prepared an all out offensive against the Baltics.

Latvian soldiers being issued with orders of the day. By mid-January 1944, the Red Army had lifted the siege of Leningrad, had gone onto the offensive and was slowly but inexorably driving the German forces westwards towards the Baltic States of Estonia and Latvia. It was in this sector that most of the Waffen-SS volunteer divisions were deployed to try to stem the Soviet drive. The main Waffen-SS force in the area was *SS.Grupppenführer* Felix Steiner's III Germanic Panzerkorps, the 11th *SS.Freiwilligen-Division Nordland* and *SS.Freiwilligen Brigade Nederland*. In addition to these volunteer divisions were the 15th and 19th Waffen Grenadier divisions from Estonia, as well as the Flemish *Langemarck* Brigade and the Walloon *Sturmbrigade Wallonien*. By the end of January, all units of the 15th Estonian Division were at full strength, consisting of 15,192 men of all ranks. However, the rear area immediately behind the front did not allow for unit training or time to learn from the combat-seasoned German troops because the Red Army immediately began heavy systematic attacks in the Novosokolniki area. (*NARA*)

Two photographs showing Latvian soldiers belonging to a *Hundesstaffel* unit during operational duties in Russia in early 1944. *(NARA)*

Latvian soldiers pulling a sled with what appears to be wicker cases containing 15cm howitzer shells. In early February 1944, part of the 15th Division was relocated to the Redya River region some 150 miles north, which was an inactive sector of the front. This was undertaken to accustom the units to combat conditions. Already the front line was under serious pressure and deteriorating. By mid-February the 15th Division was ordered to pull back to the Velikaya River region where a new defence line called the 'Panther' position was being built. *(NARA)*

A Latvian SS grenadier can be seen with locals during operations near the Velikaya River in the winter of 1944. Fighting for the volunteers was hard, and during the first four months of combat experience in Russia the 15th Division never fought as a complete unit. Even by the end of March 1944, some parts of the division had still not arrived. A drastic plan had been drawn up to accustom raw conscripts to the harsh environment of the Eastern Front and use these to support the Latvian division. However, it was soon realized that this would prove impractical because there were no longer any quiet sectors of the front. *(NARA)*

An MG 42 machine gun mounted on the Lafette 42 tripod. Although the MG 42 was an impressive weapon, often holding back an entire attacking enemy infantry regiment, it had a number of drawbacks and required a lot of attention in terms of maintenance. Dirt and battlefield debris would regularly cause jamming if left unchecked. *(NARA)*

A Latvian soldier clad in his winter reversible suit white side out is armed with a Karabiner 98K bolt-action rifle. *(NARA)*

A Latvian *SS-Untersturmführer* wearing a skin coat over his tunic and ushanka fur cap with ear flaps up. These skin coats varied greatly in size and quality and were primarily designed to be worn in extreme cold climates. They were normally worn by officers, but soldiers were also seen wearing them, especially while on guard duties. *(NARA)*

Marching Latvian SS being supported by a column of late-variant Pz.Kpfw.IVs in March 1944. By this time the divisional strength comprised 253 officers, 1,069 non-commissioned officers and 8,738 privates. Within days this strength would be bolstered by units of the 34th Grenadier Regiment, the 1st Battalion of the 33rd Grenadier Regiment and the 3rd Battalion of the 15th Artillery Regiment, giving the Latvians a well-manned division.

A soldier in a dugout in the snow armed with the MP 40 submachine pistol during February or March 1944. During this time Soviet army units carried out a number of isolated attacks in order to gain improved positions for further assaults. Over time the Russians carried out larger attacks over the Velikaya River and in March secured a bridgehead on the west bank of the river. As a result of these assaults, the 15th Division suffered heavy losses and almost lost its combat-effectiveness. *(NARA)*

Two photographs showing a Latvian grenadier whitewashing his M35 steel helmet in order to blend in well with the snow-covered terrain. *(NARA)*

A grenadier clad in his winter whites and armed with an MP 40 machine pistol can be seen here in a defensive position during the winter of 1944. Latvian units sustained heavy losses along the River Velikaya as they moved from the west bank of the river to the east bank, trying with varying degrees of success to occupy unprepared positions. *(NARA)*

Grenadiers move along a trench during defensive battles in the winter of 1944. Although the actual loss rates in the Latvian division were regarded as average during this period, the losses were perceived to be serious because there were few infantry units operationally fighting in the area. *(NARA)*

A soldier surveys the area with a pair of 6 × 30 Zeiss binoculars, trying to spot the location of his enemy hiding in the snow. *(NARA)*

From a dugout, probably at a forward observation post, this winter-clad grenadier can be seen surveying the terrain. Note the M24 stick grenade next to his position. He is also armed with an MP 40. *(NARA)*

An armed grenadier comes out of his shelter during operations in early 1944. The shelters built by the Latvians were called *Halbgruppenunterstande* (group and half-group living bunkers) by the Germans. These were to become essential for both the Waffen-SS and Wehrmacht if they were to survive the ceaseless artillery and terrible freezing weather conditions on the Eastern Front.

A Latvian soldier clad in his winter whites and armed with a Karabiner 98K can be seen walking along a shallow trench. He is more than likely on guard duties. *(NARA)*

Two Latvian soldiers both wearing the reversible winter whites and armed with the MP 40 machine pistol are more than likely on patrol duties during early winter operations in 1944.

A Latvian commander in a staff car. A Latvian could be given the position of a division infantry commander, but also served as the Latvian liaison officer to division headquarters. Under German law, only a German citizen could serve as a division commander, so while the commander was German, the subordinate commanders were Latvians who were generally well-educated and experienced officers who had served with the pre-war Latvian army. Latvian officers were assigned to serve as commanders of the division's regiments, battalions and companies.

A German doctor examines young Estonian recruits before they are conscripted into the Wehrmacht or into the newly-created Waffen Grenadier Division.

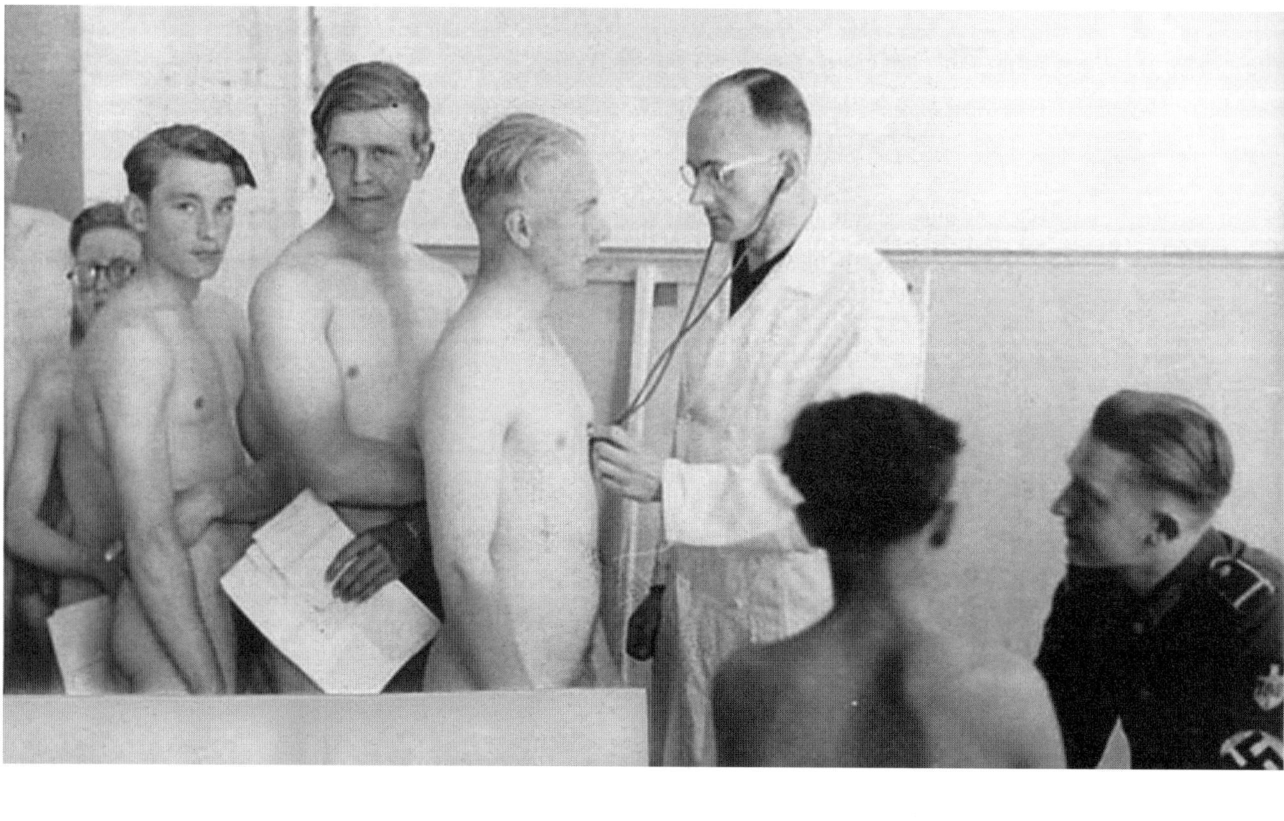

Members of the 20th Waffen Grenadier Division of the SS (1st Estonian) during operations in early 1944. The division was officially activated on 24 January 1944 and many of its soldiers had been drawn from the Estonian Legion or the 3rd Estonian SS Volunteer Brigade who had already been actively fighting with the German army.

Estonian soldiers from the 20th Waffen Grenadier Division of the SS (1st Estonian) inside a captured Russian village. By January 1944, the receding Eastern Front had been pushed back by strong Soviet forces almost all the way to the border of German-occupied Estonia. During this early period the Estonian division comprised the 45th and 46th SS Volunteer regiments and the 20th SS Volunteer Artillery Regiment. By February, as the Red Army seemed poised to invade Estonia, a general conscription was announced in Estonia by the German authorities. *(NARA)*

(**Above**) A tracked support vehicle can be seen advancing along a typical waterlogged road during defensive actions near the Estonian border. By February 1944, Estonian units under German control had about 14,000 men. The German authorities concerned about the Red Army advance on Estonia called every man to arms through any means, using both German-controlled radio broadcasts and vehicles travelling through the towns and cities to call on every Estonian to do his duty.

(**Opposite, above**) A winter-clad Estonian soldier surveys the terrain ahead using a pair of Zeiss binoculars. On 8 February 1944, the Estonian division was attached to *SS-Obergruppenführer* Felix Steiner's III SS Panzer Corps, which was defending the Narva bridgehead. The Germans had already established quite a large and strongly-defended bridgehead covering an area of territory on the eastern approaches to Narva. The defences around Narva had been fortified and hundreds of dug-in artillery positions and machine-gun nests ran from the city south along the banks of the River Narva to the shores of Lake Peipus and down to Polotsk, north-west of Vitebsk. Supporting the Estonians and the SS Panzer Corps were foreign soldiers from the SS Division *Nordland*, and Brigade *Nederland* were well dug in and all available reserves were rushed to the front line. Here foreign SS conscripts were determined to stand firm and fight in what became known as 'the Battle of the European SS'. *(NARA)*

(**Opposite, below**) A support vehicle belonging to an Estonian unit during defensive actions in the Narva bridgehead. In order to support the bridgehead, reinforcements were quickly shifted to the area including the Panzergrenadier *Feldherrnhalle*, which comprised some 10,000 troops airlifted from Belorussia. The 5th Battalion of the Panzergrenadier *Grossdeutschland* Division, including Grenadier Regiment *Gnesen*, which was an ad hoc regiment formed from replacement army units in Poland, arrived in mid-February. Three days later, the German 214th Infantry Division was transferred from Norway, and over the next two weeks various units were added to the group, including the 11th SS Volunteer Panzergrenadier Division *Nordland*, a number of Wehrmacht and Estonian units including Estonian auxiliary police. *(NARA)*

Two photographs taken in sequence show Estonian locals along the Estonian border region being relocated to safety as the Red Army slowly pushes forward. Estonian SS can be seen assisting in the operation. By early February 1944, forward Soviet units of the 2nd Shock Army had crossed the river and established bridgeheads on the west bank to the north and south of the city of Narva. The 2nd Shock Army expanded the bridgehead in the Krivasoo Swamp south of Narva five days later, temporarily cutting the Narva-Tallinn railway behind the III SS Panzer Corps. *(NARA)*

Estonian troops in early 1944. By this period in the Narva area the Estonian force comprised the 20th Waffen Grenadier Division, the 3rd Estonian Border Guard Regiment, Estonian Regiment *Reval*, 3rd Estonian Police battalions and the 2nd Estonian Eastern battalions. (*NARA*)

Soldiers can be seen being transported by halftrack during the summer of 1944.

(**Opposite, above**) Estonian soldiers during defensive operations in early 1944. During this period strong Soviet attacks were being made against the Narva bridgehead. SS Volunteer Grenadier Regiments 45 and 46 (1st and 2nd Estonian) accompanied by units of the *Nordland* Division made repeated assaults against the Red Army north of Narva. In order try to stabilize the situation, the Soviet 59th Army attacked westwards from the Krivasoo Swamp and managed to encircle the strongpoints of the 214th Infantry Division and the Estonian 658th and 659th Eastern battalions. The resistance of the encircled units gave the German command time to move in all available forces and to stop the 59th Army units' advance.

(**Opposite, below**) Two winter-clad soldiers using the bayonets from their Karabiner 98K rifles to try to detect mines in the snow laid by Soviet troops along eastern parts of the Estonian border. In spite of dogged resistance by both German and foreign soldiers, on 6 March the Russians began directing their might against Narva along the main road to Tallinn. In the air Soviet aircraft mercilessly pounded Narva while artillery from the 2nd Shock Army launched a fierce unremitting attack, firing some 100,000 shells and grenades at three weakened German regiments defending the city. However, despite the fierce attacks, after seven long weeks of fighting, the Soviet 2nd Shock Army was exhausted, low on supplies and had suffered huge numbers of casualties to mount any large-scale operations. As units withdrew along some sectors of the front to recoup, thousands of mines were laid to hinder German and foreign movement eastwards. *(NARA)*

(**Above**) Two whitewashed Sd.Kfz.251 personnel carriers halted in the snow with SS troops standing around. Note the commanding officer holding what appears to be a map. *(NARA)*

A Tiger tank during defensive operations in the Narva area in March 1944. The main brunt of the Soviet attack was to fall on Steiner's SS Korps, positioned east of Narva. The *Nordland*'s Panzer *Abteilung*, named *Hermann von Salza* and commanded by *SS-Obersturmbannführer* Paul Albert Kausch and assisted by Tiger ace *Leutnant* Otto Carius, and a platoon of four Tigers saw a number of successful engagements. Tigers also supported the SS-Grenadiers as they cleaned out the Soviet infantry. Although the crisis was temporarily averted in the centre, further north Red Army forces successfully established a bridgehead near the village of Siivertsi. To the south of the city of Narva, in the zone defended by an ad hoc army *Abteilung* named *Narwa*, Russian soldiers crossed the river and threatened to cut off Steiner's SS Korps and two Wehrmacht units. The 502nd *Schwere Panzer-Abteilung* was moved into the threatened area and quickly stabilized the German line. To strengthen the German defence the Estonian 20th Waffen Grenadier Division was rushed into the line and attached to Steiner's Korps. Steiner threw the division into battle on 20 February against the Siivertsi bridgehead. The Estonian SS soon proved themselves in combat, and within nine days of continuous fighting Red Army troops had been pushed back across the river.

Chapter Three

The Last Year 1944–45

Over the coming weeks and months SS foreign legions fought to help stem the Red Army advance. By early 1944 there was nothing but a drumbeat of defeats for the German army. It was in the Baltics where Army Group North played a decisive role in trying to curtail the rout and preventing the fragile lines from finally being smashed to pieces. As the last remnants of Army Group North were driven back across a scarred and devastated wasteland to the borders of Estonia, Latvia and Lithuania, German troops were ordered to 'stand and fight' and wage an unprecedented battle of attrition in what became known as the Battle of the Baltics.

By 2 February 1944, the Red Army was bearing down along the frontier of Estonia and threatening the city of Narva. The Germans had already established a large and strongly-defended bridgehead covering an area on the eastern approaches to Narva. Soldiers from the SS Division *Nordland* and Brigade *Nederland* were well dug in and all available reserves were rushed to the front line, which included the release of an Estonian brigade. The brigade had been drafted by the Waffen-SS, which had been since January 1944 conducting an extensive recruitment programme in Estonia, Latvia and Lithuania. Many draftees were dispirited, and their only motivation for fighting alongside the Germans was the fear of reprisals against their own people. Yet in spite of the unfavourable military situation in the Baltics, the Estonian 3rd SS Volunteer Brigade was hastily expanded into the 20th Estonian SS Volunteer Division or *20. Waffen-Grenadier-Division der SS* (*Estnische Nr. 1*), commanded by of *SS-Oberführer* Augsberger. Initially, the main fighting formations of this new Estonian division were the 45th and 46th SS volunteer regiments, and the 20th SS Volunteer Artillery Regiment. However, as the Red Army began reaching the border of Estonia, a general conscription-mobilization was announced in the country by the German authorities calling on all Estonian men to volunteer and take up arms against the Soviet army. Within weeks some 30,000 men had reluctantly volunteered themselves into the Estonian Waffen-SS. The new 20th SS Division then received additional reinforcements, bringing the total of Estonian units up to 50,000 or 60,000 men. During the whole period at least 70,000 Estonians joined the German army.

The conscription of such a large foreign force was in order to try to assist the German army in trying to defend the Baltics from the Red Army. Yet, in spite of dogged resistance by both German and Estonian conscripts, which had been attached to *SS-Obergruppenführer* Felix Steiner's III SS Panzer Korps defending the Narva bridgehead, they struggled to hold the line. Though there were isolated successes where the Estonian legions had driven Red Army units back and restored their line, the Russian force was overwhelming.

Over the next few days German and foreign SS combat formations were collapsing under a fresh Soviet assault. By 24 February the Russian spearheads had reached the main rail line supplying the Narva area, and threatened to encircle Steiner's Korps to the north. Despite heavy resistance, the Red Army pushed forward using heavy artillery and armour to smash through the German defences. *Armee-Abteilung Narwa* rushed forces south to halt the Soviet advance. A battalion from the *Nordland*'s *26. SS-Panzergrenadier Regiment Norge* was also brought south to help bolster the disintegrating line.

Despite sustaining losses and being repelled a number of times, the Russians persistently attacked all across the Narva line. Determined more than ever to crush the German defences, Russian forces undertook a heavy assault in the Lilienbach area. The area was defended by men of the *Nederland*'s 49th *SS-Freiwilligen-Panzergrenadier-Regiment de Ruyter*, commanded by *SS-Obersturmbannführer* Hans Collani, a Finnish veteran of the *Wiking* Division. Following a huge artillery duel between the *Nederland* and the Red Army attackers, the assault disintegrated into fierce hand-to-hand fighting. After several hours of ferocious combat, the Russians withdrew with huge losses. *De Ruyter* had held the line, and the Soviets decided to shift the focus of their attack elsewhere.

Over the weeks that followed, *Nederland* and Estonian forces were subjected to almost constant artillery and aerial bombardments. On the night of 6/7 March, the Red Air Force made a huge bombing raid on Narva, flattening the city. This was followed by a sustained artillery attack with hundreds of artillery pieces. The *Nederland*'s 48th *SS-Freiwilligen-Panzergrenadier-Regiment General Seyffardt*, commanded by *SS-Standartenführer* Wolfgang Jörchel, positioned to the south of *Danmark*, was attacked and forced from their positions. What followed was a ferocious counter-attack with SS troops fighting in hand-to-hand combat.

All along the German defensive line fierce fighting continued throughout March and April, with the Russians obtaining little ground against the tenacious German defenders. During this period the Red Army increased the intensity of their bombardments. On 7 March, massed Russian air attacks attempted to pulverize the German defensive positions, lasting for some twelve hours. This was followed by a large systematic artillery bombardment. However, by this stage the civilian population had already been evacuated from Narva, leaving the Waffen-SS defenders to dig deeper into the rubble-strewn streets of the city.

The main thrust of the Soviet attack was then moved against positions at Lilienbach, which was held by the Dutch volunteer regiment *De Ruyter*. Once again the SS held firm and fought to the last drop of blood. However, with huge losses in men and equipment, it soon became apparent that they would no longer be able to hold their position for any appreciable length of time.

On 23 March, Hitler declared Narva a fortress and the city to be held at all costs. However, with ammunition running low and casualties rising, the defence of Narva seemed an impossible task. Nevertheless, by early April the Germans were reprieved from the clutches of the Red Army as the spring thaw arrived, bringing an end to large-scale attacks. During April and May the front stagnated and allowed both sides to rest and regroup. By the end of May as the ground began to dry the Russians prepared their southern flank for an all-out attack against the town of Dolgaja Niva, held by the *Nordland*'s *Danmark* regiment.

On 26 May, the Estonian division was renamed the 20th Waffen Grenadier Division of the SS (1st Estonian) or *20. Waffen Grenadier Division der SS* (*Estnische Nr. 1*). The division was still under strength with some 5,000 men and as a consequence pulled out of the front line and re-formed with the recently-returned *Narwa* Battalion, which was absorbed into the division as the reconnaissance battalion. This increased the division's strength, now comprising some 15,000 men.

Throughout May and June 1944, the Narva Front continued to hold as the Russians built up their reserves for a new offensive. Wehrmacht and SS foreign legions were also attempting to bring additional reinforcements to the area in order to try to contain itself cohesively on the battlefield. Although the temporary lull had given the Germans time to build a number of new defensive positions, Army Group North was now exposed to an even greater menace that would threaten Lithuania.

On 22 June, the Russians commenced their long-awaited summer offensive against Army Group Centre, code-named Operation BAGRATION. Within a matter of weeks seventeen German divisions had been destroyed. The Soviet attack was so swift that by early July the 1st Baltic Front was now driving towards Baranovichi and then Molodechno and on to Vilnius, the capital of the Baltic State of Lithuania.

By 7 July Baranovichi was captured and the focus of effort immediately shifted to the north to Vilnius. The Russian spearhead attacked towards Slonim and Vilnius and widened the deployment of its forces, especially against German blocking units. However, German forces in the area were not going to give up ground that easily. On the Baranovichi-Berezovka road heavy fighting broke out as parts of the 4th Panzer Division halted and tried to contain Red Army units moving west along the road. The 507th *Schweres-Panzerbataillon*, the Heavy Tank Battalion, counterattacked at Leipciani, and what followed was a brutal tank battle between the battalion's Tigers and the enemy. After the successful engagement the battalion withdrew east of the Berezovka forest which enabled the Soviets to advance at breakneck speed towards Vilnius.

Already the Soviet 5th Guards Tank Army had bypassed the 5th Panzer Division, which was attempting to reach the city. Vilnius was under Hitler's 'Fortified Area' order, and the Führer had already made it perfectly clear to his commanders that it must be held at all costs. Hitler was hoping to defend the city with four Panzer divisions, but was told these could not be assembled before 23 July. It was imperative to hold Vilnius, he said, because without the city it would become a springboard for the Russians to carve their way through Lithuania on to the Baltic Sea shores and then into East Prussia. Without the city, he was concerned that it would become almost impossible to re-establish a sustainable connection between the two German army groups.

During mid-July the Battle of Vilnius raged, but as the Russians intensified the bombing of the city, it soon became apparent that the fortress could no longer withstand enemy fire. Altogether some 13,000 German troops had been killed or wounded in the defence of Vilnius, and what remained of the garrison capitulated after more than five days of continuous combat.

By late July, along the entire German Baltic Front the Wehrmacht and SS were experiencing defensive problems in many areas. The Red Army had already taken full advantage of the situation and was slowly grinding down German forces in both Estonia and Lithuania. In order to avert a catastrophe, a new defensive line was built called the Tannenberg Line (*Tannenbergstellung*) with the main defences erected to the west of Narva. Part of this defence comprised Estonian Waffen-SS.

On 24 July strong Russian forces attacked the Tannenberg Line. What followed was a series of bloodthirsty infantry and armoured battles that saw the Germans and their foreign SS counterparts dwarfed by enemy superiority. Both German and Estonian forces tried to hold their defensive positions, but in many places were pulverized by 2,000 tons of shells and grenades. The Red Army attack engulfed much of the front, but this did not deter German and Estonian front-line troops accompanied by Panther tanks and rocket artillery from launching a series of savage counterattacks of their own. Some of the counterattacks were so fierce that the Germans managed to recapture the towns of Tornimägi and Grenaderimägi.

During late July the Germans fought a number of triumphant defensive actions, trying in vain to hold the Soviets from pushing along the Tallinn highway. Although the German withdrawal to the Tannenberg Line was reached successfully by many retreating units, the city of Narva could no longer be held and as a consequence the Russians finally captured it after six long months of bloody battle at a cost of almost 500,000 men.

In the first week of August the German position in Estonia and Latvia looked increasingly grim. Army Group North was exhausted and the Russians were relentlessly driving them back by pouring troops, often manned by young boy soldiers and old men, at every weak point along the receding front. On 10 August the Third and Second Baltic Fronts launched massive air and artillery attacks against the 18th Army south of Pskov Lake and north of the Dvina. The attacks were so fierce that within only a few days massive holes were punched through the German lines, bringing fears that Estonia would soon be lost. Thousands of Germans troops were killed or wounded trying to hold back the Russian onslaught. Those that were left to defend Estonia were exhausted and undermanned.

On 17 September, General Ferdinand Schörner, commander of Army Group North, decided to evacuate his forces from Estonia before they were driven along the Baltic coast and cut off. The withdrawal was code-named Operation ASTER. It began with evacuating elements of the German and foreign formations and Estonian civilians. In less than a week some 50,000 troops and 1,000 PoWs had been removed. The remaining parts of Army Group North in Estonia were ordered to withdraw into Latvia through the town of Pärnu. As German forces retreated, the infantry was ground down in a battle of attrition and could no longer sustain itself cohesively on the battlefield. The Russians in overwhelming superiority advanced across the flat plains of Estonia using both fields and the long straight highway, bound for Tallinn. By 22 September Tallinn was captured, and two days later the Red Army heavily bombed the harbour at Haapsalu and Vormsi Island, preventing desperate German units from escaping by sea. The Russian 8th Army of the Leningrad Front then went on to capture the remaining islands off the Estonian coast in a large amphibious attack.

By the end of September, Army Group North was tactically in a more dangerous position than it had ever been. The front was badly scarred and depleted and the bulk of its forces had withdrawn from Estonia and was already being threatened in Latvia and Lithuania by deep overwhelming attacks. As the Soviets approached the border of Lithuania, drastic measures were made by grouping three or four Lithuanian *Polizei-Bataillonen* into regiment-sized units known as *Lituanische Freiwilligen-Infanterie-Regimenter*. Three such units were formed as the Soviets reached the border, and they were sent directly to the front in an attempt at holding back the Soviet onslaught. The duties of the Lithuanian units were mainly rear-area security and anti-partisan operations, with occasional front-line service. Now they were ordered in as front-line troops to help defend their country against strong Russian attacks.

However, the Red Army strength was overwhelming. From Konigsberg in the north the front had been reduced to a coastal strip of some 80 miles in width and over 400 miles in length. In the Tukums-Riga area the 5th Guards Tank Army had broken through to the coast at the end of July and was now threatening the whole area. Infantry units of Army Group North and the 3rd Panzer Army were fighting for survival and were vulnerable everywhere. The Red Army was reported to be only 35 miles from Riga to the south and 50 miles from the coast below Lake Võrtsjärv. South of Riga the SS Panzergrenadier-Division *Nordland* dug in along what was known as the *Segewold-Stellung* (Segewold position).

The Red Army's objective was to spearhead the Second and Third Baltic Fronts on a broad front towards Riga, and as the operation progressed they were to pursue *Heeresgruppe Nord* into Kurland.

With the fall of the Latvian capital came the complete evacuation of thousands of troops and 100,000 tons of materials to the Kurland bridgehead. In total some thirty divisions would be moved to the Kurland area where they were ordered to dig in and fight to the death in order to defend what remained of Latvian territory that was still in German hands. The Soviet objective was to crush the German forces and their foreign SS counterparts in Kurland, which comprised the 19th Waffen Grenadier Division of the SS (2nd Latvian) and the main body of Army Group North. The bulk of the forces in Kurland consisted of the once-vaunted German 16th and 18th armies. For the next several months the Germans bitterly contested every piece of ground in the Kurland and fought to the death.

On 25 January 1945, Hitler officially renamed Army Group North as Army Group *Kurland*, and formally designated the Kurland region as a fortress. Hitler made it quite clear that Army Group *Kurland* would not be evacuated. He was aware that there was now no possibility of restoring a new land corridor between Kurland and East Prussia. Instead, the force would have to fight to the bitter end as the Red Army commenced the encirclement and the slow reduction of the Kurland pocket. It would not be until May 1945 that the force in Kurland officially capitulated to the Soviets and the Russians were masters of the Baltic states of Estonia, Latvia and Lithuania.

Elsewhere along the receding front the Russians continued smashing their way through East Prussia, with the Soviet First Guards Tank Army finally arriving along the Baltic coast where it isolated the city of Kolberg. Defending the city were various formations from Army Group Vistula. The army group had arrived in the city days earlier after continuously fighting off heavy Russian attacks. Many of the troops were already fatigued and low on ammunition and equipment. Among the forces that arrived to defend the city were the 3rd Panzer Army, 33rd Waffen Grenadier-Division of the SS Charlemagne (1st French) and the 15th Waffen Grenadier-Division of the SS (1st Latvian). Among the defenders there were some 10,000 *Volkssturm* and *Hitlerjugend* conscripts and various other local militia and volunteers. There was an armoured gun train, eighteen tanks and a number of support vehicles of various types. Surprisingly the Germans also received supplies by air and sea, and were supported by gunfire from the pocket battleships *Lützow* and *Admiral Scheer*.

The opening attack against Kolberg began on 4 March by Soviet units of the First Belorussian Front and Second Belorussian Front. However, the first assault against the city's defences was immediately repulsed. It was not until the nearby town of Köslin was captured later that day did the Russians resume their attack against the city with additional reinforcements.

Over the next few days the Russians and Polish People's Army launched a series of heavy penetrating attacks against the city defences. The Red Army had given the Poles the task of capturing Kolberg, and it was the 3rd Polish Infantry Division along with supporting units that attempted to storm the city against heavy German resistance. Although the first Polish attack had been a courageous effort, its troops were repelled under a hail of machine-gun and mortar fire. Lightly-clad *Volkssturm* and *Hitlerjugend* were seen resisting well, and across the ravaged city they brought up the last of the ammunition to supply the front-line troops that were frantically trying to stem an enemy breakthrough. The battleships *Lützow* and *Admiral Scheer* were also supporting the defence by shelling Polish and Russian positions and helping to aid the evacuation of troops and civilians from the port.

On 12 March a new assault was launched, this time with additional armour and artillery units including the 4th Polish Infantry Division. For two days the Poles and German defenders were heavily embroiled in combat, but the Germans refused to surrender, despite incurring massive casualties.

By 15 March the Germans received additional reinforcements from the *Kell* battalions at Swinemünde, but this did not prevent the Poles from attacking the fortified positions near the railway stations and the Salt Island. The following day the battle intensified on the port and inside the city centre with heavy artillery and *Katyusha* rocket-launchers being used against strong German defences. Slowly and systematically the German defensive positions were destroyed and most of the defensive lines were reluctantly abandoned, leaving small groups of troops to hold the line while the bulk of the German and Foreign Legion forces from the city evacuated to Swinemünde.

The evacuation from the besieged city was undertaken by German naval forces in what was known as Operation HANNIBAL. Some 40,000 German soldiers were successfully evacuated from Kolberg plus around 70,000 refugees from surrounding areas. With the evacuation of the last remaining forces in Kolberg, the city finally fell on 18 March. When the Poles marched into Kolberg they found it almost unrecognizable with some 80 per cent of the city totally destroyed by heavy ground and aerial bombardment.

With the loss of Kolberg, German commanders in the field reluctantly conceded that the situation along the Baltic was so perilous that an invasion of the Reich would be imminent. Although further along the coast other ports were heavily fortified in order to evacuate, re-supply troops and contain the Red Army's remorseless drive, the loss of the Baltics had finally come to an end and the German war machine and its foreign counterparts would soon be defeated.

A group of photographs showing Estonian troops preparing to leave for the front in early 1944. Some depict soldiers saying farewell to their families, often being killed in action and never coming back to their homeland. When the recruitment programme began in Estonia volunteers had to choose between joining the Estonian SS Legion and working in war industry or as members of the military support staff. As the Red Army approached the Estonian borders, a general mobilization was announced in January 1944. Another one followed in August, which called up 17-year-old boys to join Air Force Auxiliary Services or *Flakhelfers*. The total number of Estonians in the German armed forces, including the Home Guard and the *Flakhelfers* as well as the 'Finnish Boys', was about 70,000.

eutsche
hsbahn PL

Deutsc
Reichsba
Stettin
15 792

An Estonian patrol reports in to its company commander, a Knight's Cross bearer. Even with snow on the ground, it was common for troops operating in forests to wear green and brown camouflage pattern side out, especially if the enemy was some distance off.

Estonian troops during a passing-out ceremony with their commanding officer taking a salute along the parade.

An Estonian rifle company in formation standing at ease. They are wearing the M1938 field cap or *Feldmutze* 38 generally known in the Wehrmacht as the *Schiffchenmutze* or little boat cap.

Support vehicles belonging to the 20th Waffen Grenadier Division during its divisional march to the Eastern Front in early 1944.

Troops manhandling a 10.5cm howitzer, more than likely about to connect it to a vehicle for towing. Along the front, both Latvian and Estonian soldiers found the fighting and winter conditions extremely difficult. With losses mounting, some companies panicked and left their trenches. This was especially common during an enemy tank attack or artillery barrage, which often caused considerable losses. One Latvian officer wrote in his diary on 9 March 1944 about a battle near Seredkina Slepni village and Hill 82.2. On this day the 15th Division suffered the heaviest irreversible daily loss with thirty dead and three missing. The officer outlined that the main reason for the losses was the panic that broke out among the companies of the 32nd Grenadier Regiment when they spotted four Soviet tanks and immediately left their positions and started to pull back from the east bank over the frozen river. *(NARA)*

Grenadiers mounted on half-tracks being transported from one part of the front to another. With parts of the front being lost to overwhelming enemy firepower, Latvian and Estonian forces were forced to withdraw to various sectors. With losses mounting, the inability to replace the casualties caused further problems for the units. Unlike the Wehrmacht who were often able to replace some of their losses, the foreign units had to improvise to replace theirs. This lack of replacements had a decisive impact on bringing about the collapse of the Latvian 15th Division on the Eastern Front. The higher the number of casualties, the larger the number of replacements required. However, when there were replacements rushed to plug their lines, many of the reinforcements had virtually no training experience. This in effect caused even further losses in the lines. *(NARA)*

(**Above**) Troops stand next to a crudely-built shelter constructed from straw and other surrounding vegetation. Note the discarded wooden shell crates next to the position. During late March 1944 along the Narva Front, SS and Wehrmacht units tried desperately not to fall back, in spite of being subjected to constant enemy artillery and air attacks. In other parts of the front the SS Latvian, Estonian and Danish soldiers received a heavy mauling as they attempted to try to dig in. However, as parts of the German front began to crumble the Russian Second Baltic Front stepped up its pressure against the divisions of the 16th Army, trying to punch a hole through its lines. Luckily for the Germans the weather had turned for the worse. After a warm winter, the spring thaw had set in early. A foot of water covered the ice on the surrounding lakes and Soviet tanks were sometimes sinking up to their turrets. In a number of places the roads were turned into a quagmire, making the advance painfully slow but saving the foreign conscripts from almost total annihilation. *(NARA)*

(**Opposite, above**) Troops preparing their position by laying out shells in preparation for a fire mission with their 8.8cm FlaK gun. Although predominantly built for aerial defence, this weapon was widely used as an anti-tank gun and possessed a genuine anti-tank capability. On the battlefield it proved a very versatile weapon and continued being used in a dual role until the end of the war. The 8.8cm FlaK gun was used extensively in the Narva region in 1944. *(NARA)*

(**Opposite, below**) Winter-clad soldiers can be seen during an operation in the winter of 1944.

Four photographs taken in sequence showing Latvian medical personnel assisting an injured soldier onto a stretcher. Losses within the ranks of the Latvian 15th Division were high. During the period from 1 March to 14 April 1944, the division suffered heavy casualties along positions near the Velikaya River sector. Although the losses had been very heavy, the number of casualties was not the main reason for the 15th Division's failure to retain its positions along the river. Much of the underlying reason for the collapse of the 15th Division was its total lack of training and cohesion. Many reinforcements that had been rushed to the sector had little or no training and were unable to support the lines. Even the Latvian Border Guard Regiment soldiers that were supposed to support the 15th Division lacked vital training experience. The Border Guard Regiment soldiers' average age was 33. This was regarded as significantly higher than the other soldier categories, especially within the 15th Division. Many of these reinforcements had a low level of education and were not regarded as reliable front-line infantry. As a result, these men were sent to the front to assist the 15th Division and their positions quickly collapsed with units fleeing the lines, leaving the SS to defend with no supporting arms. *(NARA)*

Two photographs taken in sequence showing Latvian motorcycle combinations, more than likely on reconnaissance crossing a makeshift pontoon. By the beginning of April the 15th Division units were gradually withdrawn from the front line, broken up as units and transferred to the rear for training. On 3 April 1944 the 33rd Grenadier Regiment was incorporated into the 13th Luftwaffe Field Division. On 5 April 1944 the VI Corps headquarters issued an order outlining the replacement of the 15th Division with the German 83rd Infantry Division. *(NARA)*

A soldier of the SS-Panzerkorps at Narva on 1 June 1944. The designation of the III Panzerkorps was composed primarily of foreign volunteer formations including the *Nordland* Division and the 4th SS Volunteer Panzergrenadier Brigade *Nederland*. The Panzerkorps had been forced back towards the Estonian frontier during the Soviet winter offensive, and the corps then participated in what was known as the Battle for the Narva Bridgehead in the summer of 1944. Throughout May and June 1944, the Narva Front continued to hold as the Russians built up their reserves for a new offensive. Both German and foreign units were also trying their best to bring additional reinforcements to the area in order to try to contain themselves cohesively on the battlefield. Although the temporary lull had given the Germans time to build a number of new defensive positions, Army Group North was now exposed to an even greater menace that would soon threaten Lithuania. *(NARA)*

Truppen of the SS-Panzerkorps at Narva in June 1944 survey one of the many bomb craters littered along the line. Note in the distance a knocked-out Russian T-34 tank. *(NARA)*

Two photographs showing a member of the III SS-Panzerkorps in the summer of 1944 near Narva. The strategic objective of the Red Army Estonian operation was to reoccupy Estonia as a favourable base for a coordinated large-scale attack against Finland and East Prussia. In order to defend Estonia, Waffen-SS units including twenty-four volunteer infantry battalions from the SS Division *Nordland*, the SS Division *Langemarck*, the SS Division *Nederland* and the Walloon Legion supported the main defence. Roughly half of the infantry comprised the personnel of the 20th Waffen Grenadier Division, which was motivated to regain Estonian independence rather than support the German war machine and the defence of the Reich.

A shirtless heavy MG 42 machine-gun crew are cleaning their weapon and the Lafette 42 tripod sustained fire-mount. In battle conditions in open terrain the MG 42 machine-gun squad would use their sustained fire-mount to protect the flanks of the advancing rifle companies. However, in built-up areas the crews often had to operate forward with the rifle platoons and in light machine-gun roles with bipods only. They were able to still sometimes take advantage of the situation and revert back to the heavy machine-gun role. *(NARA)*

Two photographs taken in the summer of 1944 on the Narva Front showing shirtless troops belonging to the III SS Panzer Korps.

(**Opposite**) Two photographs showing grenadiers from the *Nederland* Division during operations in the summer of 1944. Despite both dogged German and foreign resistance in holding their lines to the grim death, the decimation of German Army Group Centre meant that pressure now fell on Army Group North. By mid-July the Red Army had already taken full advantage of the situation and was slowly grinding down their enemy in both Estonia and Lithuania. In order to avert a catastrophe a new defensive line was built called the Tannenberg Line (*Tannenbergstellung*) with the main defences erected to the west of Narva. On 21 July Hitler grudgingly ordered his forces to withdraw to the Tannenberg Line and fight to the death. Units ordered to the Tannenberg Line consisted of strong formations made up from General Felix Steiner's III Panzerkorps. The 4th SS Armoured Grenadier Brigade *Nederland* dug in on the left north flank of the Tannenberg Line, with the 11th Volunteer Armoured Grenadier Division *Nordland* on the right south flank. *(NARA)*

(**Above**) Grenadiers of the *Nordland* Division supporting the defence of the Baltics in the summer of 1944. Much of the division by the end of June was defending the Tannenberg Line. On 24 July strong Russian forces attacked the line. What followed was a series of bloodthirsty infantry and armoured battles that saw both Germans and their foreign counterparts dwarfed by enemy superiority. Both German and Estonian forces tried to hold their defensive positions, but in many places were pulverized by 2,000 tons of shells and grenades. The Red Army attack engulfed much of the front, but this did not deter German and Estonian front-line troops accompanied by Panther tanks and rocket artillery from launching a series of savage counterattacks of their own. Some of the counterattacks were so fierce that the Germans managed to recapture the towns of Tornimägi and Grenaderimägi. During the morning of 25 July, as troops on the Tannenberg Line fought for survival, 1,360 Soviet assault guns fired almost 300,000 shells and grenades as the 2nd Shock Army began attacking across the Narva River. The remaining Estonian defensive positions that had not been blasted by the shelling were attacked, and in many areas these last strongpoints ran out of ammunition. As the Estonian troops fled in panic, they were cut down by Russian fire. Along the banks of the Narva both German and Estonian Wehrmacht and Waffen-SS forces were driven from their trenches and foxholes. As confusion swept across the entire front, commanders in the field hastily gathered the remaining units together to try to defend the main highway to Tallinn. The situation for the defenders was calamitous. The Germans were well aware how important it was to prevent the Russians advancing on Tallinn, but there seemed no stopping the Red Army drive. *(NARA)*

A Latvian machine-gun crew can be seen taking cover inside a ditch during defensive operations. *(NARA)*

Soldiers of the 23rd SS Volunteer Panzer Grenadier Division *Nederland* or *23. SS-Freiwilligen Panzergrenadier-Division Nederland (Niederländische Nr. 1)* tucking into rations. These troops were withdrawn to help assist other foreign units along the Tannenberg Line. During late July the Germans along with foreign soldiers fought a number of triumphant defensive actions trying in vain to hold the Soviets from pushing along the Tallinn highway. Although the German withdrawal to the Tannenberg Line was reached successfully by many retreating units, the city of Narva could no longer be held, and as a consequence the Russians finally captured it after six long months of bloody battle at a cost of almost 500,000 men. In the first week of August the German position in Estonia and Latvia looked increasingly grim. Army Group North was exhausted and the Russians were relentlessly driving them back by pouring troops, often young boy soldiers and old men, at every weak point along the receding front. On 10 August the Third Baltic and Second Baltic Fronts launched massive air and artillery attacks against the 18th Army south of Pskov Lake and north of the Dvina. The attacks were so fierce that within only a few days massive holes were punched through the German lines, bringing fear that Estonia would soon be lost. In a drastic measure to support the disintegrating 18th Army the Luftwaffe hastily sent a Stuka squadron to the area commanded by Major Hans Rudel, known by his comrades as the *Panzerknacker* (tank destroyer). Also the 12th Army from the remnants of Army Group Centre was ordered personally by Hitler to support the 18th Army along with a grenadier division airlifted from Konigsberg. (*NARA*)

(**Above**) Two photographs taken in sequence showing troops of the Latvian 15th Waffen-Grenadier Division moving across a field together with animal draught towing supplies. *(NARA)*

Foreign SS grenadiers crossing a field during operations in the summer of 1944. *(NARA)*

A PaK crew during a fire mission. It appears that this anti-tank crew is on a training exercise prior to being sent to the front. Various sectors of the front comprised an assortment of the 5cm PaK38, the 7.5cm PaK40, the 8.8cm PaK43 and the deadly 8.8cm FlaK guns. These guns were the backbone of the defence against Soviet armour and would prove decisive in the months that followed, despite gradual depletion of ammunition. *(NARA)*

Troops of the Latvian 15th Waffen-Grenadier Division have set up a position on the edge of a town during defensive operations in the summer of 1944. *(NARA)*

Positioned at a window is an MG 34 machine-gun crew during a defensive action. The machine gun is mounted on the Lafette 34 tripod. The optimum operating crew of an MG 34 for sustained fire operation was five men. The gunner was known as the No.1, the No.2 carried the tripod and Nos 3, 4, and 5 carried ammunition, spare barrels, entrenching tools and other items. For additional protection the No.1 and No.2 were armed with pistols, while the remaining three carried rifles. This large team was often reduced to just two or three (as in this photograph): the gunner, the loader (also barrel-carrier), and the spotter. *(NARA)*

Troops of the Latvian 15th Waffen-Grenadier Division on a march. By this stage of the war both foreign and German soldiers were fighting against numerically superior enemy forces. They were fully aware that the average Russian conscript was no longer the poorly-trained and badly-equipped conscript that had faced the mighty Wehrmacht in 1941. During the battle in the Baltics the Soviet troops now comprised experienced veterans who had excellent equipment and the latest armoured vehicles. *(NARA)*

Three photographs taken in sequence showing a Latvian light MG 34 machine-gun crew preparing their defensive position. When times and conditions allowed, machine-gun crews invariably prepared a number of fall-back positions. They appreciated the full value of the MG 34, and along these fall-back positions the machine-gunners were able to set up advantageous defensive positions. In the face of the mighty Soviet Army time and time again SS units stood firm against almost impossible odds. Even some of the most fanatical SS troops fighting in the Baltics must have realized that military success was now impossible, yet they continued to make sacrifice after sacrifice, often holding the lines with a few MG 34 and MG 42 machine-gun positions in order to allow other units to withdraw. *(NARA)*

A column of T-34 tanks advancing along a road in Lithuania. Supporting the tanks' drive are infantry, two of which are armed with the PTRD-41 anti-tank rifle. Although this weapon was unable to penetrate the frontal armour of a German tank, it could pierce the thinner sides of lighter-armoured vehicles such as thinly-armoured self-propelled guns. With the situation further deteriorating for the Wehrmacht, the Red Army exploited Army Group Centre's position by making wide outflanking moves north driving its powerful 1st Baltic Front towards Baranowicze and then Molodechno and on to the city of Vilnius, the capital of the Baltic State of Lithuania. The attack was known as the Vilnius offensive and was conducted by units of the 3rd Byelorussian Front. They were opposed by the remnants of the 3rd Panzer Army and the 4th Army.

(**Above**) Young soldiers marching during operations in Kurland. Both German and Latvian forces were given the task of defending Fortress Kurland. The Germans and their Latvian allies had barely dug into their lines in mid-October when the Soviets attacked. The main Red Army drive, which amassed two Soviet Army corps with thirteen divisions, targeted the weak part of the fortress against the Latvians. For days shells and gunfire rained down on the Latvians, but they stood firm. Tank after tank was brought to a flaming halt along with the infantry. Surviving soldiers kept running forward, shouting wildly to keep the momentum going. By 22 October the Russians, savagely mauled by the determined defence, fell back. The Soviets had underestimated the strength and determination of their enemy. Further attacks on Kurland were mounted on 27 October, but still the Russians could not breach the outer defences. Soviet commanders were optimistic that it would only be a matter of time before Kurland would be crushed. This engagement would continue until the end of the war. Both German and Latvian soldiers were dug in deeply.

(**Opposite, above**) Latvian soldiers can be seen with one of their support vehicles which has inevitably slipped off an icy track. The principal objective of the Red Army in January 1945 was for an all-out assault along the Baltic and to crush the remaining under-strength German units that had once formed the vaunted Army Group North. German forces were slowly becoming compressed along the last remaining strips of land along the Baltic shore of Latvia and Lithuania. With every defeat and withdrawal came an ever-increasing pressure on the commanders to exert harsher discipline on their weary men. Although the defence of the Baltic States automatically stirred emotional feelings for the Latvian and Estonian forces to fight for their land, not all soldiers felt the same way. In some sectors of the front, commanders in the field found that many conscripts, especially those newly-recruited, began showing signs that they did not want to die for a lost cause. Conditions in the Baltics were miserable, not only for the newest recruits but also for battle-hardened soldiers. For the majority of these troops they had been forced to withdraw along the shores of the Baltic Sea in a vain effort to defend it to the last man. *(NARA)*

(**Below**) An Estonian winter-clad grenadier armed with the Panzerfaust and the MP 40 is seen on the march through the snow. For Germany, stemming the Soviet winter offensive in 1945 was no more than a short reprieve. By February, it no longer had enough small arms to equip newly-conscripted foreign soldiers in the Baltics, and as a result losses were high. German, Estonian and Latvian troops were now barely holding their wavering lines with what ammunition and supplies they had left at their disposal. *(NARA)*

A whitewashed Tiger tank can be seen rolling through the snow supported by winter-clad grenadiers during the winter of 1944.

Inside a forest and an assault gun crew poses for the camera in front of the *Sturmgeschütz* (StuG) during a lull in the fighting. By 1944 the *Sturmgeschütz* had become an extremely common assault gun, especially on the Eastern Front. By this period of the war the StuG had been slowly absorbed into panzer units, panzer and Panzergrenadier divisions of the Wehrmacht and Waffen-SS.

A blurred image as two soldiers belonging to the Latvian 15th Waffen-Grenadier Division are preparing to move hastily through a town. They are both wearing their summer camouflage tunics. *(NARA)*

Well-camouflaged soldiers in a defensive position in a slit trench. Much of the front consisted of many miles of trenches and various other forms of defensive positions. Although the Battle of the Baltic States of Estonia, Latvia and Lithuania was almost over by early 1945, what was left of Army Group North withdrew into East Prussia, Pomerania and Silesia to begin the last defensive action before the Reich. *(NARA)*

Two Latvian grenadiers armed with bolt-action rifles are seen in a staged defensive position. They are well concealed inside a 'foxhole' and their helmets have foliage attached in order to break up their headgear's distinctive shape from enemy ground observation. *(NARA)*

A group of injured soldiers comprising mainly the Latvian 15th Waffen-Grenadier Division can be seen after being treated in a field hospital. *(NARA)*

Chapter Four

The End

By December 1944, the 20th Waffen-SS Grenadier Division was almost destroyed during heavy unrelenting fighting. The strength of the division was significantly reduced as many Estonian troops were released from German service and the remaining troops were evacuated from Estonia to the Neuhammer training grounds, where the formation was reconstructed from October onwards. The division was re-formed and totalled some 11,000 Estonians and 2,500 Germans. These troops were returned to front-line duties in late February 1945 as the Red Army launched its long-awaited Vistula-Oder offensive. This offensive was fierce and within days German and Foreign Legions were pushed back behind the Oder and Neisse rivers. Heavy fighting continued and the division found itself trapped with the XI *Armeekorps* in Silesia. By February, the division was so depleted that it was renamed as an ad hoc *SS-Kampfgruppe*. Over the coming days and weeks the *Kampfgruppe*'s sole intention was not to defend its positions any more but to escape from the Russian onslaught. In desperation to escape complete decimation, the *Kampfgruppe* left all its heavy weapons and equipment behind and remnants of the division moved south around the Goldberg area. They eventually capitulated near Prague with many of them executed on the spot by Czech partisans. The remaining Estonians fled and reached the Western Allies, but were then handed back to the Russians.

As for the 15th Waffen-SS Grenadier Division, it had fought mercilessly around Leningrad, where the division had been forced to withdraw through the Baltic States. Depleted and under-strength, surviving elements of the division were sent by boat to Danzig where the division fought on the Pomeranian Wall defences. It then retreated through Pomerania and in Germany where an ad hoc *Kampfgruppe* fought in the defence of Berlin. What was left of the *Kampfgruppe*, comprising some 824 men under *Waffen-Standartenführer* Vilis Janums, surrendered on 27 April 1945 to the advancing Americans at Güterglück near the River Elbe. The remnants of the division, amounting to some 4,500 men, surrendered to the Americans south of Schwerin on 2 May 1945.

The 19th Waffen Grenadier Division of the SS (2nd Latvian) had meanwhile been fighting desperately while trapped in the Kurland Pocket. Red Army forces launched six major offensives against the German and Latvian forces entrenched in the Kurland Pocket between 15 October 1944 and 4 April 1945. The German 4th Panzer Division, 31st, 32nd and 93rd Infantry divisions, 11th SS Division *Norland* and remnants of the battered and bruised infantry divisions of the 218th, 227th and 389th including what was left of the 15th Latvian SS Division were evacuated over the sea. Eventually, approximately 135,000 German troops surrendered in the Kurland Pocket on 12 May 1945. Some 180,000 German troops were taken into captivity from the Baltic area and the majority of these PoWs were initially held at the Valdai Hills camps.

Appendix I

Order of Battle

15th Waffen Grenadier Division of the SS (1st Latvian)

19th Waffen Grenadier Division of the SS

20th Waffen Grenadier Division of the SS (1st Estonian)

15th Waffen Grenadier Division of the SS (1st Latvian)

Waffen Grenadier Regiment of SS 32
Waffen Grenadier Regiment of SS 33
Waffen Grenadier Regiment of SS 34
Waffen Artillery Regiment of SS 15
Waffen *Füsilier* Battalion of SS 15
Waffen *FlaK* Battalion of SS 15
Waffen Signals Battalion of SS 15
Waffen *Pionier* Battalion of SS 15
Waffen *Panzerjäger* Battalion of SS 15
SS Medical Battalion 15
SS *Nachschub* Troop 15
SS *Feldpost* Department 15
SS Veterinary Company 15
SS *Wirtschafts* Battalion 15
SS *Bau Regiment* 1 of 15. SS-Division
SS *Bau Regiment* 2 of 15. SS-Division
SS *Feldersatz* Battalion 15
SS Waffen *Feldgendamerie* Troop 15
SS War Reporter Troop 15

19th Waffen Grenadier Division of the SS

Waffen-Grenadier Regiment SS 42 Voldemars Veiss
Waffen-Grenadier Regiment SS 43 Heinrich Schuldt
Waffen-Grenadier Regiment SS 44
Waffen-Artillery Regiment 19
SS-*Füsilier* Battalion 19
SS-*Panzerjäger* Unit 19

SS-*FlaK* Unit 19
SS-Pioneer Battalion 19
SS-*Nachschub* Troop 19
SS-*Sanitäts* Unit 19
SS-*Feldpostamt* 19
SS-*Nachrichten*-Unit 19

20th Waffen Grenadier Division of the SS (1st Estonian)

45th SS Volunteer Grenadier Regiment
46th SS Volunteer Grenadier Regiment
47th SS Volunteer Grenadier Regiment
20th SS Volunteer Artillery Regiment
20th SS *Füsilier* Battalion
20th SS *Panzerjäger* (Anti-Tank) Company
20th SS Engineer Battalion
20th SS Anti-Aircraft Battalion
20th SS Signals Battalion
20th SS Divisional Supply Troops

Each grenadier regiment consisted of three battalions, and the artillery regiment consisted of four battalions: three equipped with 10.5cm leFH 18 howitzers and one with 15cm sFH 18 heavy howitzers.

Appendix II

Army Group North June 1944

Reserves
12th Panzer Division

SIXTEENTH ARMY

Reserves
24th Infantry Division
69th Infantry Division
281st Security Division
285th Security Division

I Army Corps
205th Infantry Division
87th Infantry Division

X Army Corps
389th Infantry Division
290th Infantry Division
263rd Infantry Division

II Army Corps
81st Infantry Division
329th Infantry Division
23rd Infantry Division

VI SS-Corps
15th SS-Grenadier Division 'Latvian.1'
19th SS-Grenadier Division 'Latvian.2'
93rd Infantry Division

L Army Corps
218th Infantry Division
132nd Infantry Division
83rd Infantry Division

EIGHTEENTH ARMY

Reserves
215th Infantry Division

XXXVIII Army Corps:
21st Luftwaffe Field Division
32nd Infantry Division
121st Infantry Division

XXVIII Army Corps

30th Infantry Division
21st Infantry Division
212th Infantry Division
126th Infantry Division
12th Luftwaffe Field Division
1st (Estonian) *Grenzschutz*-Regiment
2nd & 3rd (Estonian) *Grenzschutz*-Regiments (attached to 227th Infantry Division)
4th (Estonian) *Grenzschutz*-Regiment
5th (Estonian) *Grenzschutz*-Regiment (attached to 207th Security Division)
207th Security Division & 5th (Estonian) *Grenzschutz*-Regiment

ARMY 'NARVA'

Army Reserves

61st Infantry Division

XXVI Army Corps

227th Infantry Division & 2nd and 3rd (Estonian) *Grenzschutz*-Regiments
170th Infantry Division
225th Infantry Division

XXXXIII Army Corps

58th Infantry Division
11th Infantry Division
122nd Infantry Division

III Panzer Corps-SS

SS-Panzergrenadier Division *Nordland* & SS-Grenadier Brigade *Nederland*
20th SS-Grenadier Division 'Estonian.1'

***Kustenverteidigung* 'West'**

2nd Luftwaffe *FlaK* Division & 5th (Estonian) Battalion

***Kustenverteidigung* 'West'**

285th Security Division & 4th (Estonian) Battalion

Appendix III

Formation of Army Detachment 'Narva'

III SS (Germanic) Panzer Corps – *SS-Obergruppenführer* Felix Steiner
11th SS Panzergrenadier Division *Nordland*
4th SS Panzergrenadier Brigade *Nederland*
20th Waffen Grenadier Division of the SS (1st Estonian)

XXVI Army Corps – General Anton Grasser
11th Infantry Division
58th Infantry Division
214th Infantry Division
225th Infantry Division (Wehrmacht)
3rd Estonian Border Guard Regiment (as of 15 April 1944)

XXXXIII Army Corps – *General der Infanterie* Karl von Oven
61st Infantry Division
170th Infantry Division
227th Infantry Division
Feldherrnhalle Panzergrenadier Division

Gnesen Grenadier Regiment
Separate units
Eastern sector, coastal defence (staff of the 2nd Anti-Aircraft Division as the HQ) – Lieutenant General Alfons Luczny
Estonian Regiment *Reval*
Three Estonian police battalions
Two Estonian eastern battalions
Other military units
Artillery Command No. 113
High Pioneer Command No. 32
502nd Heavy Tank Battalion
752nd Anti-Tank Battalion
540th Special Infantry (Training) Battalion

In the summer of 1944, the Panzergrenadier Division *Feldherrnhalle* and seven infantry divisions were removed from the Narva Front.

Notes

Notes

Notes

Notes

Notes

Notes

Notes

Notes

Notes